M000283092

FORGOTTEN
TENNESSEE

BACKROADS AND ROADSIDE SURPRISES

JERRY JCL WINNETT

AMERICA
THROUGH TIME®
ADDING COLOR TO AMERICAN HISTORY

America Through Time is an imprint of Fonthill Media LLC
www.through-time.com
office@through-time.com

Published by Arcadia Publishing by arrangement with Fonthill Media LLC
For all general information, please contact Arcadia Publishing:
Telephone: 843-853-2070
Fax: 843-853-0044
E-mail: sales@arcadiapublishing.com
For customer service and orders:
Toll-Free 1-888-313-2665

www.arcadiapublishing.com

First published 2019

ISBN 978-1-63499-152-0

Typeset in Trade Gothic 10pt on 15pt
Printed and bound in England

CONTENTS

ABOUT THE AUTHOR

JERRY WINNETT is a photographer, painter, and designer. He is not an author, so to speak; however, he is a storyteller and enjoys an audience. He loves his tales of abandoned places, and relishes tales of roadside surprises. There are few things he gets a kick out of more than telling his listeners about exploring an empty house filled with children's toys and rotting floors. Are these tales true? Are they fabrications? Since he is a photographer, he is able to show his audience photographic proof of his tales from the forgotten.

FORGOTTEN TENNESSEE
CAPTURING THE PAST AS IT FADES

For those of you who are new to Forgotten Tennessee, let me introduce myself. I'm Jerry Winnett, a photographer who one day looked at his work and decided to take a different path. Before Forgotten Tennessee, I produced my work under Jerry Winnett's Grindhouse Photography. Grindhouse consisted of photographing beautiful women in broken down and gritty locations. I liked the work, but it had its ups and downs. While most models showed up for their shoots, when they didn't, I'd be left with a gritty, broken down location and nothing to do but shoot the building. After a while, I realized this was fine. After all, buildings, if they did not fall prey to fire or developers, would always be available to shoot.

My fascination with shooting empty buildings came from the fact that no building or location is truly abandoned. People still frequent them and leave evidence of their passing, such as bottles of beer, graffiti, trash, campfires, and more.

Not all of what you find in this book will be a building forgotten by time and people. I will also be including shots of what I call "roadside surprises"—old tractors, memorials, and yes, even an airplane cockpit.

A Boat in a Grassy Field

I was driving the backroads of an area in Rutherford County, Tennessee, near Shelbyville Highway. I'd been wanting to explore this area and had finally gotten around to it. The road I was driving down meandered with many curves and had at least one bridge that narrowed down to one lane, and judging by the bashed-in guardrail, at least one driver had dragged their vehicle across its surface. Further

down the road I hit a straight away. I'd been driving around 15 mph and had yet to run across another driver, when I passed a boat. More specifically, a sailboat in a field—and damn if it didn't look like it was trying to hide behind a hedge.

THE BLACKMAN CEMETERY

When I began Forgotten Tennessee, I started by getting lost—a lot. At the time, the area I lived in was not heavily developed and there were still plenty of backroads available. It was off I-840 that I feel I really began my documenting of Forgotten Tennessee. I used to drive to Columbia, Tennessee from Murfreesboro, Tennessee, quite often. On the way back, I could see on the left side of I-840 two massive trees that were separated by what looked like the stone foundations of a massive house that had at some point fallen into ruins. I drove by this site many times, until I decided to find the access road so I could take a better look at these ruins. Imagine my surprise when I finally discovered my mysterious trees and stone foundations were sitting in the middle of a farmer's field that, luckily for me, was allowed to go fallow.

The gate was an iron thing pitted and gone over with the rust of long decades.

I was looking at a cemetery that had been purposefully forgotten: Blackman.

I didn't know it at the time, but I'd found the burial ground of Esquire Alfred Blackman, one of the founders of Murfreesboro, Tennessee. Alfred Blackman had come Tennessee in 1808 and acquired quite a bit of land. After setting up a general store a blacksmith, he eventually petitioned for the building of a U.S. Post Office.

To say the least, I was shocked that I'd found myself walking through the burial ground of such a historically renowned family, a burial ground apparently was forgotten by many of Murfreesboro's residents. I'm not sure how long I spent in the Blackman cemetery but while there I captured what I could and left with a feeling of peace.

ALFRED BLACKMAN
Born in
Sampson Co. N. C.
Nov 14, 1790.
Moved to
Rutherford Co. Tenn
in 1808.
Married to
Elizabeth Crawford,
In 1809,
Became a disciple of
Christ in 1812.
Died June 29, 1872.
Aged 81 y's. 7 mo. 15 d's.

A LONELY PLACE TO REST

Elam Road, near Ransom Mill Dam is mostly dirt, pot holes, and rocks. A natural ceiling of overhanging tree limbs makes for a perpetual twilight. It's quite memorable. Unfortunately, people have used the sides of the road as a dumping ground for TVs, couches, cabinets, and mattresses. I'd was pretty disgusted and was about to write the place off as having nothing worth shooting when a bright spot of color caught my eye. Markers like this can be found on roadsides throughout Tennessee, close to an accident where someone has died. This one, however, was 12 feet into the woods. I've visited this marker several times since my initial discovery. The surrounding flora are kept trimmed away from the memorial, and new flowers are placed there often.

Tennessee State Prison, Nashville, TN

One particular gray and blustery day I found myself wandering around West Nashville's industrial area. Before I knew it, I came across the entrance to the Tennessee State Maximum Security Prison that had been closed since 1992. Driving by I could see a guard shack and a gate. The shack was empty, and the gate was up. I turned my car around and drove by two more times before pulling up and honking my horn to see if anyone would stick their head up. Instead, I was greeted by silence. Figuring that fortune favors the brave, I threw caution to the wind and drove in.

I'd hidden my car in an empty lot on the property and spent the afternoon wandering the grounds. I walked into one prison yard after another, shooting away. I should have been happy with the photos I'd taken, but I wanted to get inside the prison and shoot. Eventually I found a small guard house and knocked on its door, which was a big mistake. Said big mistake was a guard who stood 7 feet tall, 3 feet wide, and was one of the largest men I'd ever seen.

I quickly decided that parking in front of the prison was a bad idea. Instead, I drove alongside a long wall until I found a yard to hide my car.

I took a moment to admire the beautiful architecture of such a horrid place.

From there, I spent the next few hours shooting to my heart's content.

I watched the vultures
flock to land on the
guard towers, just
to take right back
off minutes later. I
wondered how many
prisoners wished they
could have done the
same.

The surprised guard did not look in the least bit happy to see me, and when I asked if there was any way I could shoot inside the prison, I received a loud, resounding, "No." The guard then wanted to know how I'd gotten onto the grounds. I detailed my entrance and my photographing of the prison grounds. The guard became even unhappier looking with me (shocking, I know). I was then informed that I had exactly "ten seconds to get out of his sight, or I'd see the inside of a cell, all right." I'm pretty sure my car's tires left scorch marks on the asphalt from the speed of my departure.

STRANGE BIBLE

I come across strange things. One of the strangest was a bible I'd come across in an abandoned house in the Blackman Community of Murfreesboro. The house itself was nearly hidden above an embankment that required a bit of effort to climb.

On this particular adventure, I was accompanied by a model friend named Tiffany who was wanting to do a vampire-esque shoot. Walking in, we found a room that had a mattress, suitcases, and many books cast about the floor. Curious about the books, we picked one up and discovered it to be a bible of sorts—one filled with creepy illustrations depicting war, strife and pain. The good news was the bible went perfectly with our shoot.

GLUM HOUSE

Cruising down a side road off of I-840, I noticed the tall peak of a barn with a vulture on it. How could I resist photographing and exploring such a place? I pulled into the spot and made my way toward an old barn and its house.

The barn was a cornucopia of old textured wooden surfaces, hay matted floors, and multi patinas upon any visible metal.

Left: It was a sweet hat, but I opted not to try it on.

Below: Just as I turned, I noticed something I'd almost missed: a house lost behind tall grasses. Without a second thought, I plowed through the grass and made my way to the house. Glum was the only word I had for the house.

But while some might find that off-putting, I found it compelling, so in I went. Once in, I could see what had once been a kitchen and bathroom. The bathroom floor had collapsed so I avoided it, but I didn't avoid the other rooms.

BURIED BY THE FLOOD

In 2010, Nashville, Tennessee, almost washed away in a flood of epic proportions. The damage went into the hundreds of millions of dollars and more than a few people died. Ten years later, evidence of the severity of the flood are starting to make their way to the light of day.

AND WE'LL NEVER BE ROYALS (OR GUESTS)

There are few locations that I consider to better examples of "forgotten gold" as a hotel that has closed its doors. I've shot three so far, including the Howard Johnson's in Nashville and the Eldorado, also in Nashville. Both were amazing to shoot, but unfortunately, they ended up victims to the wrecking ball. On this day, I was in Springfield, TN. While driving around, I passed a defunct hotel called the Royal. My heart went all pitter-patter!

Doors hung ajar down the wings of the Royal, on both floors. Rooms still had furniture inside: beds, tables, TVs, etc. Some even had small kitchens. Trash was also plentiful, and a few TVs sat outside of their rooms, all proof that the Royal still had guests even if room service was on permanent hold.

Below: Yeah, the pool was a bit small, and I'd certainly not recommend diving in at any depth.

There is a chill I feel when I cautiously enter a room whose bed has obviously been slept in, and where every available surface is littered with empty beer or soft drink bottles. I find myself wondering if someone is still there. Will they be coming back? Are they somewhere out of sight watching me? Places like this should be frightening, and they are, but they emit such an aura of mystique that one is able to kick fear to the curb.

Ivy Consumes

Out towards Rockvale, Tennessee, there is a house sitting back from the road. It's old to say the least, and it is being consumed in ivy.

The ivy has spread from the tree in the front yard, carpeting the porch and beyond.

HIDDEN ON OLD NASHVILLE HIGHWAY

Old Nashville Highway is a highway that I'd driven up and down more times than I can count. The highway cuts through the Stones River Battlefield in Murfreesboro, Tennessee, and for the longest time I honestly thought that the battlefield and its vast cemetery were the only real points of interest. I was wrong. It turns out that after the Civil War, some of the Union Army's African American soldiers decided to settle in the area. They built houses, planted fields, and lived their lives. I would have never known this if someone had not bush-hogged the highway. The construction was stone, adobe, and wood. All of it was falling apart and it all called to me to come and explore.

The porch was dominated by a couch and two doors, one peppered with buckshot.

Keeping an eye out for roots and tangles of debris, I walked on up to the newly revealed house and marveled at the fact that a multi-roomed structure like this had been hiding in plain sight.

Unfortunately, the house was on its last days, and it was literally falling down in places. I was happy I was able to capture it before time and the elements could wipe it out forever.

EVER SEE A HOUSE THAT JUST SCREAMS "HAUNTED"?

Yeah, I've seen a few of those. But this one I came across in Auburntown, TN, was the scariest. On top of the creepy looking trees that bookended the grey and rust colored house, the smell of decomposition from a deer carcass was enough for me to motor on.

Is That a Head?

In Nashville, there was once an abandoned hotel called the Eldorado. I was photographing Dale Rainey, a model friend, at the hotel. We had moved from the main building to an adjacent wing enclosed by a concrete freeze. Almost upon entering the hall, we stopped dead. Maybe 25 feet from us was a round, hairy object. We slowly approached the thing. The closer we got, the slower we crept.

Unkempt hair stood out at angles and we could clearly see the sallow, pale skin of a neck.

Clutching one another we slowly inched closer to the mysterious object. Using the toe of one shoe, I kicked the hairy thing over. We both screamed. A face stared back at us. The face of a mannequin's head!

RESTLESS ON I-40

I woke up restless one morning and felt the need to travel. I grabbed my cameras, fueled up my car, and hit US I-40 East. The miles rolled by and eventually they grew more numerous than my fellow travelers—or at least it felt that way. I began to relax and realized this was exactly what I'd been needing. Climbing uphill, I spied a defunct gas station named STOP and decided a bit of exploration was in order. I smiled at the name. I wasn't sure when this place pumped its last gallon of gas, but it had certainly been a while. There was a payphone in the parking lot, and a small pill box of a building next door.

I walked around the store that originally caught my eye and shot what I could, but sadly realized that without a crowbar I'd not be shooting Stop's interior.

Crouching down, I entered the neighboring building through a severely shattered glass door. Walking around, I decided that whatever this place had been, it finished up as a curio shop selling second-hand goods.

Scattered about were old audio tapes, while in another corner sat a bunch of old CRT monitors—dinosaurs, to say the least. On my way out, I looked at a family photo album. I had to wonder what became of the people inside of it. How did it end up on top of an ancient 70s-era television in a dead store?

A large wooden console TV from the 70s or 80s sat on the floor, as did an old stereo with a dual cassette deck.

STOOPED IVORY

On one of my trips I found myself in Auburntown, Tennessee. What caught my eye was a small, dilapidated, red clapboard house. It was barely standing up and on the porch stood an equally distressed stand-up piano. As I shot the two, a little white-haired black man came out and introduced himself. It turns out the house had been his auntie's where he and his nine brothers and sisters grew up. The piano was their only entertainment.

THE WORLD'S LARGEST TREEHOUSE, CROSSVILLE, TN

Getting to the treehouse requires taking a narrow road and one that is not in good repair. At the end of this road I was greeted by very large sign that did not welcome visitors. After a bit of hunting, I found a way into the grounds.

The 10,000-square-foot construction is in the *Guinness Book of World Records*. This local attraction was once an easy-to-find tourist spot. A preacher named Horace Burgess had originally built the treehouse after he said God had commanded him to do so. Burgess had begun construction of the treehouse in the 1990s, but unfortunately it closed in 2012 at the orders of the local fire marshal.

Right: A staircase led upstairs to unknown sights. And while it looked safe, I decided not to take them.

Opposite: A bit of walking takes you into a copse of trees, and through them you get glimpses of the immense treehouse.

Above left: Carvings like these dot the grounds.

Above right: At the end of this ramp is another ramp, one that had dry rotted and collapsed.

The color of the wood contrasts so beautifully with the green of late summer growth. I was happy I came out.

68

Nature Eats an Earth Mover

I've always thought machines like bulldozers to be impervious to nature's wear and tear, until I came across this bulldozer, which nature had hungrily reclaimed.

THE SPRINGFIELD GLASS FACTORY

One of my all-time favorite places to shoot is the Springfield Glass Factory in Springfield, TN. Originally, the glass factory was a wool mill. I first heard of this location from Dale Rainey, who'd been in a White Stripes video shoot there.

The mill/glass factory will always have a soft spot in my heart. I only wish I could shoot it every day.

I fell in love with the place from the moment I laid eyes on it. I ended up shooting the mill several times, with models and without.

AND ON YOUR LEFT, A DAIRY BARN AND AN AIRPLANE!

Yes, a cockpit from a plane was sitting next to a dairy barn. I had no choice but to take the nearest turn and double back to make sure I was not seeing things. I was happy I did. This is the kind of roadside gold I love finding.

I DIDN'T KNOW.

"I didn't know that there was a graveyard under the Church St. bridge!"

That was my amazed declaration one night when a friend told me about a cemetery his girlfriend had shown him the previous weekend. I live in Murfreesboro, Tennessee, and have lived there for over two decades. I really thought I knew this area. One of the major roads in and out of Murfreesboro is Southeast. Church Street. Southeast Church is a long road and one that has a bridge that spans an industrial area and railroad tracks. Now, I've been on this stretch of road thousands of times, and you would think I would have noticed the graves below it at some point—but I hadn't. I needed to check this out.

My hunt led me down a road (several actually), until I spotted a grave in a vacant lot next to an empty lot of a truck rental place and a church. I drove my car further along the parking lot and found, between two small hedges, an entrance to a weed choked expanse of land that shared space with a young forest. As I approached the young forest, I spied one grave marker, then another, and another. There were dozens! And within the forest were even more headstones and markers.

With camera in hand and a cup of hot coffee, I took to the road and went in search of this mysterious cemetery.

Some headstones were toppled, while others were ensconced by dead vines, weeds, and tree roots. I was awestruck. I spent the next few hours wandering the small forest, shooting what I could. At one point, I came to a clearing where there were even more headstones. I walked around, going down into small dips and up onto rises. It was later I realized that the dips I had stepped into were collapsed graves.

I continued my exploration and was appalled that this graveyard had fallen into such disrepair. The most recent grave I had found was dated in the 1960s, while the oldest was almost 150 years older. There were expensive looking headstones and ones that were as humble as you could imagine.

I finished shooting and that day posted my work on my original site, jwinnettcreative.com, and on Facebook. I was thrilled to learn from viewers the name of the cemetery and some of its history. According to James Allen Gooch, the cemetery I'd rediscovered belonged to the African American Benevolent Society. The one I'd shot was #11. The actual name was likely the Benevolent Lodge #11 and was founded in the late 1890s. The grounds were large enough to allow for almost 1,000 entombments, which included Buffalo Soldiers and soldiers who served in the Spanish American War and World War I. Many buried on the grounds were cared for and then buried by members of the Benevolent Lodge. You can read more about them at www.rutherfordtnhistory.org/benevolent-cemetery-re-dedication.

I realized, however, with a bit of sadness, that the dips and rises were graves whose coffins had, over time, collapsed.

ROADSIDE POOL

This roadside pool is one of my favorite shots. It was taken during an exploration of Red Boiling Springs, Tennessee. The pool is so quaint and randomly placed, and yes, I could see myself hanging out there and drinking a beer or two.

I could see myself sitting at the head of this pool in the early eve, just enjoying the simple life.

TAKE ME OUT TO THE OLD BALL FIELD!
NASHVILLE'S GREER STADIUM

In 2018, Jay Farrell and myself teamed up to shoot the former home of the Nashville Sounds, Greer Stadium, which had been abandoned since 2014. We wanted to see how hard it would be to gain entrance and we wanted to see how the old stadium had held up over time. After a bit of investigating, I learned of an access point to Greer, and on an overcast day with gear in hand, we set off. We circled the fence surrounding Greer until we found a hole in it, and in we went.

We found ourselves on the left side of the Nashville Sounds outfield, right next to the wall. I took a couple of shots of the Sounds' giant guitar score board and then we moved forward to the infield. Once there, we moved on into the stadium itself. The dugouts were grim and parts of the floor were crumbling. The tunnels leading beneath them were too dark and dank smelling to explore—this time, that is. Next time we'd bring flashlights.

Moving up to the risers where the general public would have sat in plastic chairs, we could see that even here, the ravages of time were evident. Large cracks could be seen throughout the concrete and in places steel sheets had been placed to cover up missing sections of the concrete floors.

We climbed to the seating level of the stadium, and into the main wings. Here, crowds would have entered in order to reach their seats. These tunnels were dark, but not too badly lit, and of course they were wonderfully tagged in graffiti. From there, we took the fire stairs to the second level of the stadium, where we found ourselves in the wings that lead to the second-floor consisting of business offices and the main restaurant.

Finally, we had made it to the best seat in the house, the club suite. From right to left, every wall was tagged and we were treated to the most impressive view from the top of Greer Stadium. From here, Jay and I made our way along the left wing of the stadium and back. After a while we exited the way we had come in.

All in all, Greer was a treat to shoot, and we'd have to come back and explore the lower tunnels and rooms that we could not enter due to a total absence of light. Remember this, folks: you shoot what you can, and if you still want more, then come back better equipped! It's better to come back than find yourself injured or dead.

Everywhere we could see the marks of squatters, vandals, bored teens, vagrants, artists, and more. Graffiti was everywhere, and nearly all the floor to ceiling windows had been shattered in, the glass crunching under our feet.

Right: Looking down onto the bleachers. There were bikes, bottles, shopping carts, and other odd bits of junk.

Below: Entering the private suites was done by stepping through holes that had been knocked through, dividing panes of glass. This sounds easy until you realize that a misstep could mean a 20-foot drop to the seats below.

Forgotten Tennessee Explores an Alabama Asylum

To kick off 2019, Jay Farrell and I took a trip down to Tuscaloosa, Alabama, to photograph the Old Bryce Insane Hospital, an infamously haunted and abandoned site. After many false leads, we found ourselves in Northport, Alabama, traveling down the driveway of the Old Bryce Insane Hospital. The driveway was narrow, overgrown, and in a horrid state of disrepair. Halfway down the road, we noticed we were not alone. A large SUV was approaching us, and we wondered if we were busted. Was this trip going to end just as we'd found our destination? No. The SUV that approached us was driven by two guys who were just out enjoying some off-roading.

Finally, we hit the end of the drive and climbed out of our car, in a circular driveway. A battered mattress and trash littered the entrance. After a quick equipment check of our cameras, we took a moment to take in the size of the structure we'd spent hours driving to find. Oddly enough, in the background, we could hear the rumble of more off-road vehicles.

"We should have brought flashlights."

The lobby was dark, but we could see walls that had been tagged with graffiti, while others were demolished. Decorative red tile covered the floors along with garbage, cans, bottles, and bricks. Slowly walking over the piles of rubble, we made our way to the center of the lobby where we took a second to look around. On the far right and left of the main building were wings for patients, while in the middle another wing stretched off. Since the middle wing was slightly better lit than the other wings, we chose to explore it first.

As we made our way down the center wing, we peeked inside the open cells.

The Old Bryce Insane Hospital has been empty since 1977, and looking at the several inches of dirt on the floor, I believed it. Little if any glass remained in the windows of the wings of the building. Water dripped constantly down on our heads as we moved towards a back wall. It was here we found a stairwell whose outer wall had been torn open. The stairwell looked like skeletal remains peeking out from a rotted body. Feeling more than a little wary, Jay and I decided to chance going up the stairwell to continue our exploration.

Below: Shattered bricks, tree limbs, tiles, and garbage made the going tricky, to say the least.

On each floor, we discovered dormitory-like bathrooms and showers, only one of these still sported a heavy porcelain bathtub. Running down the center of some of the wings were wooden tracks. I'd love to know what their purpose was. Did these tracks come with the building? Were they added for deconstruction purposes?

We were wanting to go to the third floor, but the upper interior stairwells were looking worse than the first set we had climbed, so we went up the exterior stairs instead. While I'm not too afraid of heights, the view down through the stairs grating made my mouth go dry and my toes cringe. Sure, the stairs felt sturdy, but so did a floor I once went through. However, this is just par for the course.

At the top of the third-floor stairs stood a rusty door that looked as if it had suffered from a bomb blast. Twisted out of shape, it allowed us room to enter, but here we balked. The previous floors had been dirt encrusted, uneven, and strewn about with tiles and bricks. This floor looked much, much worse. Saplings and bushes were growing on the its surface. With no telling if there were weak spots that might collapse beneath us, we decided not to enter.

We took the exterior stairs to the first floor and then entered the left wing through an empty window. On the way down, we had considered exploring the basement, but nixed the idea since we hadn't brought any means of lighting our way beyond our phones. Later, we did find a staircase leading into that basement, but it was in even worse shape than the others we'd seen.

Jay and I went back down to the second floor for a bit of exploration then we would check out the outer wings of the hospital.

In the back of the main building we discovered a way into the basement; however, there was one problem. The basement was flooded. How deep was the water? It didn't matter. We weren't going swimming today.

Having explored the main building, Jay and I followed a path to the out buildings behind the Old Bryce. Here there stood three buildings: the first was made of brick, and its doors stood open. Inside was a large, airy room containing a few pieces of furniture such as an old wheelchair leaning on its side. Other pieces sat here and there as well as a few soggy mattresses.

An iron smoke stack had collapsed on the roof of the next building. Inside stood a pair of gigantic furnaces, both at least twelve feet tall. On the back walls of the furnaces were small tunnels that may have been for loading in coal or for digging out ashes. In yet another room were two equally giant boilers, and leaning over it all was the mouth of the iron smoke stack that had destroyed the tin roof.

Over the next few days, Jay and I looked further into the history of the site we'd explored. It turned out the Old Bryce Insane Hospital was in the downtown area of Tuscaloosa, Alabama. The location we'd explored was in actuality the Jemison Center, the Alabama State Farm Colony for Negroes. It was eighty-eight years newer than the original Bryce, but for whatever reason, people in the area called it the Old Bryce Hospital and the name stuck.

In 1939, the Jemison Center had been built upon the remains of a Southern Plantation purchased by the state of Alabama. The era was a sad time for America.

The Great Depression was still gripping America while Jim Crow and segregation were the law of the land. The Jemison Center was a segregated institution made to ease the population demands put upon the Bryce Insane Hospital. The Jemison Center also had another, more sinister purpose: to keep the ghost of slavery alive. All of the Jemison's African American inmates were made to labor in the fields of the old plantation for free. The oppressive creepiness that permeated the Jemison was now explained.

While the continued existence of slavery was depressing to learn, it is still history. Exploration of places like the Jemison Center lead to questions. If you go deep enough, you may learn their answers. You're richer for it.

FINAL NOTE

One of the motivations behind Forgotten Tennessee is the simple act of discovery and to preserve memories of the past. I hope you've enjoyed the photos and the stories included in this book. There will be another, I hope. Until then, I will be traveling those backroads, coffee and camera in hand.

BIBLIOGRAPHY

Benevolent Society

http://rutherfordtnhistory.org/benevolent-cemetery-re-dedication/

The Old Bryce Insane Hospital

Tom Kirsch & Opacity.us

https://opacity.us/site245_jemison_center.htm

https://en.wikipedia.org/wiki/Bryce_Hospital